UtG

Generally, the most vocal of Bible critics are people who are relaying snippets of information they have picked up from others, without reading "The Good Book" for themselves. Possibly some of the issues that these folks have raised with you are dealt with in this book. While probably coming under the genre of "apologetics", its style and level make it understandable for each of us. It provides us with valuable explanations of biblical concepts that may be regarded as incompatible with the fact that we present a God who has loved the world and desires the salvation of all. These insights will give us helpful material as we try to encourage people to regard "The Good Book" as the inspired Word of God. A valuable addition to your evangelistic "weaponry"!

Jack Hay (*Bible Teacher*)

Just because you have come to believe that the Bible is God's Word, doesn't mean you have become confident in its every part, and perhaps especially in those parts that seem so odd, so harsh, or so confusing. This little book is meant to help—and it will help! It will help you better understand how God's goodness and grace suffuses every page of His precious Word.

Tim Challies (*Author of Seasons of Sorrow: www.challies.com*)

This is a helpful and accessible introduction to some of the hard questions Christians will be asked about moral issues and matters of choice as we engage with contemporary culture. Useful answers are provided and other good sources of reading are identified. A valuable resource for young and old!

Ian Burness (*Former General Director of Echoes International*)

This is an excellent book, dealing with some of the so-called moral objections raised against the Bible. These are candidly faced and clearly answered. Paul demonstrates that some of the difficulties asserted in the Old Testament arise due to misunderstanding of the biblical text and what it describes or teaches. A real strength is that contemporary issues are faithfully discussed, e.g., the roles of men and women in church and family, and homosexuality. The scriptural position on them is explained and upheld. Read it if you are enquiring about the gospel. Read it if you are a young Christian; it will strengthen both your faith and your confidence to witness in current Western culture.

Alan Gamble (*Bible Teacher*)

With *The Good Book* Paul McCauley gives a helpful introduction to some of the difficult issues in Scripture. The topics covered are relevant, and McCauley's interaction with them is clear. For both students and sceptics of the Bible, *The Good Book* is a great resource and prompt for further study.

Dr Paul Twiss (*Associate Professor of New Testament, The Masters Seminary, California*)

THE GOOD BOOK

THE GOOD BOOK

PAUL McCAULEY

THE GOOD BOOK BY PAUL McCAULEY

Published by *Understanding the Gospel*
Typesetting and Design by *Words to World*
Book Cover by *Stephen Mullan*

ISBN: 978-1-78798-898-9 (print)
ISBN: 978-1-78798-899-6 (eBook)

British Library Cataloguing-in-Publication Data
A catalogue record for this book is available from the British Library.

Printed and bound in the United Kingdom by BookVault.

10 9 8 7 6 5 4 3 2 1
28 27 26 25 24

CONTENTS

FOREWORD

Every Christian is called to be an ambassador for Jesus Christ in this world, and that involves more than living a different life and showing kindness to our neighbours. It entails engaging in conversation with people about the message of the Bible, and that will inevitably mean from time to time having to attempt to field strong objections, such as, "doesn't the Bible condone genocide?" or, "how can you trust a God who is homophobic?" The answers to objections like this may well not be sitting at the forefront of our minds and, at worst, we can be discouraged from witnessing again. At best, they require a bit of thought before attempting to give an answer, and by that time the moment has probably passed.

For as long as I have known him, I would describe Paul McCauley as a student of Scripture. From university days, into employment, and then on to full-time Christian ministry, involving evangelism and Bible teaching, Paul has always had a keen interest in understanding the Bible and unpacking its truth for the benefit of others. In recent years, his experience of "boots on the ground" evangelism has brought him into contact with all sorts of objections to the relevancy and integrity of the Bible.

In my own experience, people who raise the difficult questions will not generally be interested in a detailed study of, for example, slavery in the Bible. Brief, informed, and thought-provoking answers are called for, and it is for this reason that I recommend reading this short book. It will give you answers which are usable in your everyday life and witness.

In succinct chapters, Paul addresses issues such as slavery, cruelty, genocide, homophobia, and other similar objections to the "Good Book". The publication is not intended to be an exhaustive study of these subjects, but the concise answers provided should help to give us confidence in the living Word of God as we take its life-giving message to a lost world.

Stephen Grant

PREFACE

These chapters were originally blog posts for the *Understanding the Gospel* website. I wrote them for three main reasons:

1. These are issues I had encountered from unbelievers as I engaged in evangelism. They had been fed a distorted view of the Bible, and, because of that, they weren't even prepared to give the gospel a hearing. Dealing with these issues was necessary to clear the way for the gospel.
2. These are issues I had encountered from believers. There were Christians who were greatly troubled by certain passages. They were rocked in their confidence in Scripture and robbed of their enjoyment of it. I have no doubt there are many believers who struggle with these issues but are afraid to voice their concerns for fear of being judged as unspiritual, or because they don't want to burden others with their difficulties. They put up a façade, but there is a rot underneath that will eventually result in the façade collapsing. It is important that we don't

pretend these challenges don't exist, because the world certainly isn't prepared to make that pretence.

3. These are issues I had encountered myself. I have felt the fear, discomfort, and sometimes even panic, as I have read certain sections of Scripture. I understand why people struggle. But these are "understandable misunderstandings". There are answers to the problems.

I have leaned heavily on the research of Paul Copan, and his book *Is God a Moral Monster?*.[1] For a more in-depth treatment of these issues I direct readers there. What I have tried to provide here is a shorter, simpler response that will help you think through some troubling passages and give you a framework for thinking about any other tough texts you may encounter.

My thanks to all who have helped and encouraged. To Eleanor Rogers for editing the blog posts, to those who gave encouraging feedback, to the UtG team for their input, to Stephen Grant for writing the foreword, and especially to the Christians who have confided in me and asked for help with these issues – I count it an honour to be asked, and it is to them this book is dedicated.

---

[1] Paul Copan, *Is God a Moral Monster? Making Sense of the Old Testament God*, Baker Books, 2011.

THE STARTING POINT

It used to be that the Bible was known as the "Good Book", and those who rejected it did so because they saw it as presenting too high a moral standard. Society has changed. Many reject the Bible now because they think it presents too low a moral standard. They say that the Bible and those that believe it are evil.

One of the loudest and most eloquent critics of Scripture is Richard Dawkins. In his best-selling book, *The God Delusion*, he said:

> *The God of the Old Testament is arguably the most unpleasant character in all fiction: jealous and proud of it; a petty, unjust, unforgiving control-freak; a vindictive, bloodthirsty ethnic cleanser; a misogynistic, homophobic, racist, infanticidal, genocidal, filicidal, pestilential, megalomaniacal, sadomasochistic, capriciously malevolent bully.*[2]

---

[2] When Dawkins was accused of cherry-picking and presenting a simplistic view of God, he immediately conceded the point, saying, "I accept that, of course . . . It was semi tongue in cheek actually." premierchristianradio.com/Shows/Saturday/Unbelievable/Episodes/Unbelievable-Richard-Dawkins-debates-Old-Testament-morality.

When Christians hear this kind of attack, the immediate impulse is to be on the defensive, and go through each charge showing that God is not guilty. But before presenting our defence, let's ask what kind of a court is this? Who is the judge and what is the law?

Dawkins is a materialist – he believes that the only reality is physical reality. But that implies there is no such thing as good and evil in an objective sense – there are just things that you like or don't like. Evil is a departure from the way things ought to be, but in a godless universe there is no way things *ought* to be. Dawkins is the one who said, "The universe that we observe has precisely the properties we should expect if there is, at bottom, no design, no purpose, no evil, no good, nothing but blind, pitiless indifference."[3] If, at bottom, there is no evil and no good, then his complaint about the Bible being immoral is groundless.

Only if this universe came from a morally good God can there be such a thing as evil. And only the Bible presents a God who can be morally good. Morality has to do with interactions between persons. That means that if God were a single, solitary person, He could not be good by nature – He wouldn't have been good in the absence of creatures. But the Bible presents God as a trinity of persons – He has always existed in relationship, meaning that moral goodness is essential to His nature. If we reject

---

3   Richard Dawkins, *River Out of Eden: A Darwinian View of Life*, Basic Books, 1995, p. 133.

the God of the Bible, we have no foundation for anything being good or evil.

So, the starting point in any discussion about the morality of the Bible is, "By what standard?" By what standard does someone condemn God and His Word, and why is that standard binding?

The person who rejects the God of Scripture has nowhere to stand to make his accusations.

But maybe the person raising the objections isn't an atheist. Maybe you are a Christian. You know God is the only foundation for morality, but as you read certain passages of Scripture it seems God is condemned by His own standard. The Bible presents God as good but you are bothered by sections that appear to present Him doing or condoning things He elsewhere condemns as evil. I know the feeling. I have been there.

I remember sitting with a young Christian who was in tears because of something that he read in the Bible, and he said, "That just seems so messed up." In our conversation we did get to the specific problem, but I didn't go straight there. There were a few things I wanted to set out first of all.

First, there is abundant evidence that the Bible is the Word of God. The many fulfilled prophecies of Scripture, its amazing unity and its life-transforming message all stand as proof that the Bible is not an invention from men but a revelation from God. If the Bible is God's Word, then it means that whatever it teaches is true. If the God of Scripture does something, then it is right, and if He allows something, He has a good reason. We can trust, even if we don't understand.

Second, when we read the Bible, we are reading about cultures that are very different from ours. So, we need to make sure we have correctly grasped both the *intent* and the *content* of the passage. Sometimes a passage reports things without condoning them, indeed, sometimes it reports them in order to expose the evil of them. This is the case, for example, with polygamy. Some people think that, because the Bible records great men of God having more than one wife, it is supportive of the practice, but that misses entirely the intent of those passages. Everywhere polygamy is seen in Scripture we see harm coming from it. The Bible isn't supporting it, it is undermining it – that's the *intent*.

Also, we can misunderstand the *content* of a passage. This is particularly true with biblical slavery. We import notions of slavery from the more recent past into the ancient past and equate the two. As we will see, they are not the same.

Many of the problems we have with things we see in Scripture are due to the influence the biblical gospel has had on the world. God was working in a world in which life was cheap and hard. The spread of Christianity has had such a positive effect on morality everywhere it has gone that we look back with horror at the way things were. We need to be "culturally aware" and get our historical bearings.

Third, God has been fully and finally revealed in Christ. If we want to know exactly what God is like, we look at Jesus. He gives us the entire story and the complete picture. As Rico Tice put it, "When we look at Jesus, all the guessing games about God stop." Looking at Christ shows us a God who is infinitely good and can be completely trusted.

With these things established, we can go to the problem passages and horror texts without panic – there are answers.

So, let's get into the specifics.

ABRAHAM & ISAAC

Genesis 22 is a chapter that puzzles and offends many people. God tells Abraham to sacrifice his son; Abraham is about to do it, then God steps in and stops it. Why would God be so cruel to Abraham and Isaac? What does it say about a God who would ask for such a thing, or Abraham who would do it? What would a Christian do if God asked the same of them? Do Christians think it's noble to kill your son if God says to? Can God command anything? If we isolate the chapter from its biblical and historical context then it understandably leads to these troubling questions, but that's not because we've understood what's going on; rather we've misunderstood.

To understand this incident, we need to see it in light of Abraham's present, his past and his future.

ABRAHAM'S PRESENT

Child sacrifice was something that many ancient religions practised. If people had heard that Abraham was going to sacrifice his son there wouldn't have been shock and horror. God took Abraham to the brink and stopped him to show to him vividly that Yahweh does not want human sacrifice. He is different from the tribal deities around Abraham, and the great nation that would come from Abraham would be different from all the nations around, and would not sacrifice their children.

The sacrificing of children was one of the reasons God expelled the Canaanites from the land in the days of Joshua (see Deuteronomy 18:9-14). God told His people they were to have nothing to do with such "abominations".

The revulsion we feel as we consider child sacrifice is a product of the influence of the Bible. Child sacrifice has been practised by almost every culture historically, and tragically it is still practised in our "enlightened" culture. Every day, thousands of children are sacrificed on the altars of abortion clinics to the great god of "choice". If someone supports this, then their condemnation of the account in Genesis 22 seems more than a bit hypocritical.

I have heard atheists challenge Christians by asking, "Would you sacrifice your son if God told you to?" And they are missing the point. Genesis 22 isn't saying God might ask you to sacrifice your son; it is saying He never will. That's not the kind of God He is.

ABRAHAM'S PAST

God was not testing Abraham's love but his faith. God had told Abraham that the great nation that would bless the world would come through Isaac (Genesis 17:19,21).

Was Abraham prepared to trust God even when he didn't understand?

Earlier, Abraham, at Sarah's insistence, had been prepared to send his other son, Ishmael, out to what would have been certain death. God gave him a promise that He would preserve Ishmael (Genesis 21:12-13). Abraham had trusted God with his less favoured son, but would he trust Him with his beloved son? The whole experience was also going to give Abraham a taste of the heartache that Hagar (Ishmael's mother) experienced as a result of his actions.

Abraham did trust God to work things out. In verse 5 Abraham showed that he fully expected to come back down the mountain with Isaac again. Hebrews 11:19 tells us that he reckoned God was going to raise Isaac from the dead. He knew somehow it would all work out, because God had promised.[4]

ABRAHAM'S FUTURE

This incident was a picture of something that would happen in the future. As Paul said in Romans 8:32, God "did not spare His own Son, but delivered Him up for us all". Genesis 22:2 gives us the first mention of love

---

[4]   It's worth noting as well that Isaac wasn't a little boy. In verse 5 Abraham calls him "the lad" but this is a word that is translated elsewhere in Genesis as "young man", e.g., 14:24; 18:7. It is also used of Ishmael in chapter 21 when he was in his teens. The point is: Abraham who was well over 100 could not have offered Isaac unless Isaac had been willing. Isaac was trusting God to fulfil His promise too.

in the Old Testament, and it is the love of Abraham for his son. It is no coincidence that the first mention of love in the New Testament is the love of God the Father for His Son: "This is My beloved Son, in whom I am well pleased" (Matthew 3:17). The Lord Jesus said that Abraham was given a revelation of the coming Messiah (John 8:56) – it could well be that Mount Moriah was where that happened. He learned, "I don't have to give my son for God; God is going to give His Son for me." "For God so loved the world that He gave His only begotten Son, that whoever believes in Him should not perish but have everlasting life" (John 3:16).

When you extract Genesis 22 from its setting, it is a challenging chapter, but seeing it in the context of Abraham's present, past and future puts it in a vastly different light. Rather than it being a source of embarrassment for Christians, it is a source of wonder and a cause for worship.

SLAVERY

One of the things that people understandably object to is that slavery seems to be condoned in the Bible. There are instructions in both the Old Testament and the New Testament on how to treat slaves. Why would God allow such an evil practice?

Here are three things to keep in mind:

GOD'S PROTOTYPE

God's original plan for mankind is seen in Genesis 1 and 2 – man and woman living in harmony together, in fellowship with God, as stewards of His creation. God created human beings in His image, meaning that they have inherent and infinite value, and are not to be treated as means to ends. They are not commodities. He states that creation is given for man to use, but humans aren't given for us to use. This shows right away that slavery is not God's intention. In fact, when you look at the creation stories from the ancient religions, the gods created humans as slaves – they were created to do the dirty work the gods couldn't be bothered doing. The Babylonian creation myth, *Atrahasis*, says:

When the gods instead of man
Did the work, bore the loads,
The gods' load was too great;
The work too hard, the trouble too much . . .
Belet Ili the womb goddess is present –
Let her create primeval man
So that he may bear the yoke.

It is no surprise then that slavery arose from cultures with that worldview.

Slavery is something that issued from the fall and man's sin; it is not something that issued from creation.

GOD'S PROHIBITIONS

In the Mosaic Law, God forbids stealing and selling humans. In fact, anyone who engaged in human trafficking was to be put to death:

"He who kidnaps a man and sells him, or if he is found in his hand, shall surely be put to death" (Exodus 21:16).

This is confirmed in the New Testament. In 1 Timothy 1:9-11 Paul puts kidnappers in the same list as murderers, fornicators and others, as those whose behaviour is opposed to "sound doctrine" and contrary to the "glorious gospel of the blessed God".

Furthermore, the Lord Jesus taught us to love our enemies (Matthew 5:44) and do to others as we would have them do to us (Matthew 7:12).

These verses unequivocally condemn the whole enterprise of the slave trade.

So, what was going on in the Old Testament when God gave instructions regarding slaves? We have to try to rid ourselves of the notion that this is the kind of slavery that existed in the southern United States. The slavery in the nation of Israel was indentured service. If you were in over your head in debt or had robbed someone, you could put yourself into the employ of your creditor or victim and work for him, getting your lodgings and food in his home. The servant was to be regarded as a hired worker, not a mere slave (Leviticus 25:39-40). At the end of the seven-year period of servitude he could go free, with sufficient resources to stand on his own two feet (Deuteronomy 15:12-15).[5] People in our society condemn this as primitive and harsh, but it is a great example of reparative justice. Is our system that puts the offender in prison at greater expense to society really better?

In terms of foreign servants, the land of Canaan was given by God to the nation of Israel (to provide a place for the arrival of the Messiah for the blessing of the world).

---

[5] The servant was to be given the option of release at the end of seven years, but every fifty years in Israel there was the Year of Jubilee, which was a great reset when land was returned, debts forgiven, and servants released. If the Year of Jubilee came before the seventh year of service, the servant was to be released.

15

So, only Israelites were allowed to own land. If foreigners wanted to live in the Israelite community then they had to be incorporated into a home, and the only way poor foreigners could do this was by selling themselves into servanthood. As we have seen, the Israelites were explicitly forbidden to steal anyone for slavery. There were regulations to ensure their humane treatment, and when these regulations are compared with how other ancient Near Eastern cultures treated slaves (see, for instance, the Code of Hammurabi), the contrast is stark. The strangers in the land were not to be oppressed and the reason God gives for this is that He loves them (Deuteronomy 10:18-19).

GOD'S PROGRAMME

God's original plan was that humans would live in harmony with God and each other. Sin spoiled the relationship between God and man, and marred the relationships that exist between humans. Man became self-centred and, rather than looking for ways to serve others, wanted to be served – thus slavery arose. And slavery was a universal fact. Every culture engaged in it.

God's programme for the world is to restore that harmony – to bring about a world in which slavery will not exist. But God was working with real people in the real world. The Lord Jesus shows us this in Matthew 19. He is asked a question about divorce, and He takes them back to the beginning, showing them that God's original plan is one man and one woman becoming one flesh for life. They then asked Him, "Why then did Moses command to give a certificate of divorce . . . ?" (v.7). The Lord replied, "Moses, because of the hardness of your hearts, permitted you to divorce your wives, but from the beginning it was not so" (v.8). Notice, the civil law of Moses does not express God's ideal arrangements for society.

To illustrate the point, let's assume that human activity is causing real damage to the climate, and the only way to save the planet is to go back to agrarian societies – no cars, no factories, etc. There is no way such a massive change could be implemented in one leap. It would have to be done step by step. Similarly, the Mosaic law makes provisions for practices that were so imbedded in human activity that it just wasn't practical to eliminate them all at once. The Mosaic law put up safeguards, made improvements and changed attitudes. It was progress on the journey.

When we come to the New Testament, the slavery that existed was not a Christian invention – it was Roman slavery. Timothy Keller writes:

> [T]here was not a great difference between slaves and the average free person. Slaves were not distin-guishable from others by race, speech or clothing. They looked and lived like most everyone else, and were not

17

segregated from the rest of society in any way. From a financial standpoint, slaves made the same wages as free labourers, and therefore were not usually poor. Also, slaves could accrue enough personal capital to buy themselves out. Most important of all, very few slaves were slaves for life. Most could reasonably hope to be manumitted within ten or fifteen years, or by their late thirties at the latest.[6]

This is not to defend Roman slavery, but merely to understand it. It was not "slavery" as we think of it, i.e., New World slavery. Those who take issue with the New Testament giving instructions to slaves and masters really need to get into the real world. If Paul had commanded all Christian slave owners to free their slaves, or if he had commanded all slaves to rise up against their masters, what would have happened? Slavery was such a part of Roman life that crucifixion was the punishment for a disobedient slave. The best place for a slave to have been in that society was with a Christian. For Paul to call for the overthrow of this institution would have been taken as an act of revolution, would have resulted in a lot of bloodshed, and wouldn't have got rid of slavery.

Instead, what Paul did was subvert slavery and show that it is antithetical to Christianity. He says in Galatians 3:28 that, "There is neither Jew nor Greek, there is

[6]   Timothy Keller, *The Reason for God, Belief in an Age of Scepticism*, Hodder & Stoughton, 2008, p. 110.

neither slave nor free, there is neither male nor female; for you are all one in Christ Jesus."

Slavery was, therefore, an evil in society that the advance of the gospel and the Christian worldview would eventually eliminate, and so it did. Where the gospel prospers, slavery can't survive.

When the Lord returns, He will bring all creation into "the glorious liberty of the children of God" (Romans 8:21), and slavery will be forever gone. In the meantime, He is setting people free from the worst slavery of all – slavery to sin – and He is doing it through the gospel. "Therefore if the Son makes you free, you shall be free indeed" (John 8:36).

GENOCIDE

Another subject that causes people to think the Bible is an immoral book is the slaughter of the Canaanites in the time of Joshua. It is portrayed as an act of genocide – a tribal deity commanding ethnic cleansing. The image is disturbing, but it is distorted.

Before clarifying and explaining what happened, let's get rid of this notion of genocide and ethnic cleansing. The issue was not the ethnicity of the people in the land of Canaan. God has always been interested in the blessing of the whole world. Indeed, His special relationship with the nation of Israel was with the intention of the blessing of all nations (Genesis 12:3). We saw in our chapter about slavery that God "loves the stranger" (Deuteronomy 10:18).

Let's lay out a few factors that need to be kept in mind as we consider the destruction of the Canaanites.

THEY WERE WICKED

The book of Genesis lays a foundation that shows that God is not swift to judge. In the time of Noah, there was no one outside of his family with any regard for God or righteousness. Later on, Abraham knew that God was a righteous judge who would not destroy the righteous with the wicked. In fact, God would have spared the evil cities of Sodom and Gomorrah if there had been ten righteous people in them (see Genesis 18:17-33). This was established hundreds of years before the conquest of Canaan and needs to be kept in mind. Added to that, God was prepared to wait about 430 years (even though it meant the Israelites were slaves in Egypt) because the sin of the Canaanites had not yet reached its limit (Genesis 15:16). Only when the society had reached its tipping point did God move in judgement. This makes it clear that God views these large-scale judgements as a last resort.

It is clear from Scripture that the Canaanites were guilty of unspeakable wickedness. For example, Leviticus 18 refers to all sorts of sexual sins and child sacrifice, and says that the Israelites aren't to engage in such practices, "for by all these the nations are defiled, which I am casting out before you. For the land is defiled; therefore I visit the punishment of its iniquity upon it, and the land vomits out its inhabitants" (vv.24-25; see too Deuteronomy 18:9-14).

But lest anyone thinks that the Bible is libelling the Canaanites to justify Israel's actions, there is evidence outside of Scripture that shows that God was certainly not exaggerating. Ancient papyri testify to the sexual perversions of the Canaanite nations, and Plutarch reports that during Canaanite sacrifices, "the whole area before the statue [of Molech] was filled with a loud noise of flutes and drums so that the cries of the wailing should not reach the ears of the people." According to UCLA researcher, Shelby Brown, "No other ancient people . . . regularly chose their own children as sacrificial victims".[7]

It is not the case that the Canaanites were living in peace and paradise before the Israelites came. The land flowed with milk and honey, but there were also a lot of tears and blood mixed in.

THEY WERE WARNED

This was not a surprise attack on unsuspecting nations. They had advance warning that the Israelites were coming. The Exodus from Egypt, the defeat of Pharaoh's army at the Red Sea, and the battles that took place on the way to the Promised Land were all known to the inhabitants of the land. This is made clear by what Rahab said to the two Hebrew spies (Joshua 2:9-11):

> I know that the Lord has given you the land, that the terror of you has fallen on us, and that all the inhabitants of the land are fainthearted because of you. For we have heard how the Lord dried up the water of the Red Sea for you when you came out of Egypt, and what

---

[7]   Clay Jones, *We Don't Hate Sin So We Don't Understand What Happened to the Canaanites*, https://clayjones.net/wp-content/uploads/2011/06/We-Dont-Hate-Sin-PC-article.pdf. I refrain from going into more detail, but the disgusting, degrading practices of the Canaanites are on record, as Jones shows.

you did to the two kings of the Amorites who were on the other side of the Jordan, Sihon and Og, whom you utterly destroyed. And as soon as we heard these things, our hearts melted; neither did there remain any more courage in anyone because of you, for the Lord your God, He is God in heaven above and on earth beneath.

The right response to this display of God's power would have been repentance and unconditional surrender. The Old Testament testifies to the fact that this always results in mercy (see, for example, Jeremiah 18:7-8 and the book of Jonah).

THEY WERE WARRIORS

The cities that were destroyed in the book of Joshua were, according to archaeological evidence, not civilian populations, but military strongholds. "That means that Israel's wars here were directed toward government and military installments; this is where the king, the army, and the priesthood resided. The use of 'women' and 'young and old' was merely stock ancient Near Eastern language that could be used even if women and young and old weren't living there. The language of 'all' ('men and women') at Jericho and Ai is a 'stereotypical expression for the destruction of all human life in the fort, presumably composed entirely of combatants.' The text doesn't require that women and young and old must have been in these cities."[8]

THEY WERE WELCOME

The experience of Rahab shows that the Canaanites were welcome to become part of God's covenant community. They could have repented of their wickedness and renounced their idolatry. Rahab was received into the nation, and even became part of the promised line from which the Messiah came (Matthew 1:5).

THEY WERE WITHDRAWN

The language of destruction and slaughter is used, but it is often used in a context in which expulsion from the land is clearly meant, for example, Deuteronomy 9:3-5:

> *"Therefore understand today that the Lord your God is He who goes over before you as a consuming fire. He will destroy them and bring them down before you; so you shall drive them out and destroy them quickly, as the Lord has said to you.*
>
> *Do not think in your heart, after the Lord your God has cast them out before you, saying, 'Because of my*

---

[8] Paul Copan, *Is God a Moral Monster?*, p. 176. The only women likely to be in such places would have been those in the same profession as Rahab.

righteousness the Lord has brought me in to possess this land'; but it is because of the wickedness of these nations that the Lord is driving them out from before you. It is not because of your righteousness or the uprightness of your heart that you go in to possess their land, but because of the wickedness of these nations that the Lord your God drives them out from before you, and that He may fulfill the word which the Lord swore to your fathers, to Abraham, Isaac, and Jacob."

When Moses spoke to the Israelites before they entered the Promised Land he told them how they could enjoy God's blessing in the land and also warned them of the conduct that would result in their expulsion and exile. In his summing up and final appeal he said, "I call heaven and earth as witnesses today against you, that I have set before you life and death, blessing and cursing; therefore choose life, that both you and your descendants may live" (Deuteronomy 30:19). The point he was making is that life is synonymous with enjoying the blessing of the Promised Land.

Moses held out to the people life and death, blessings and curses, and urged them to choose life – which meant, quite specifically, living in the promised land as opposed to being sent into the disgrace of exile.[9]

---

[9]   N. T. Wright, *The Resurrection of the Son of God*, SPCK, 2003, p. 92.

Thus, being put out of the Promised Land is called death and described as destruction. The Lord's intention was the cleansing of the land from the defilement of the nations. It needs to be remembered as well that God warned the Israelites that if the Israelites followed the path of the nations then the same fate – exile from the land – would be visited on them, and it was. So, the language of complete destruction of every living thing is ancient Near Eastern rhetoric for complete victory, and what was demanded by God was eviction, not annihilation.[10]

CONCLUSION

God is the author of life and has the right to take it whenever He sees fit. He is also the source of moral value, and as such, everything He does is, by definition, right, even if we don't understand it. In addition, these were instructions that were given for a specific occasion, and there is no normative command to engage in physical warfare in God's name. He used the nation of Israel as His instrument of judgement on the evil Canaanites (just as He used the Babylonians as His instrument of judgement against the Jews centuries later). This shows there was no genocide, there was no ethnic animosity. There was righteous recompense on wicked and unrepentant nations. It is still terrifying, but "Aslan is not a tame lion."

---

[10]   For more on this, see Copan, *Is God a Moral Monster?*.

"Aslan is a lion – the Lion, the great Lion." "Ooh" said Susan. "I'd thought he was a man. Is he quite safe? I shall feel rather nervous about meeting a lion" . . . "Safe?" said Mr Beaver . . . "Who said anything about safe? Course he isn't safe. But he's good. He's the King, I tell you." (C. S. Lewis, The Lion, the Witch and the Wardrobe)

HOMOPHOBIA

Culture has shifted, and shifted fast. In 2015 in the USA, same-sex marriage was declared a constitutional right and legalised in all 50 states. The President, Barack Obama, was an enthusiastic supporter of this, but when he was running for his first term in 2008, he said he believed marriage was between a man and a woman, and was not in favour of same-sex marriage. To say such a thing now is to declare yourself a dinosaur, a bigot and a hater.

Here in the UK in 2021, the Labour leader, Sir Keir Starmer, visited a church in London which ran a foodbank, ministered to the poor, and had opened its premises to be used as a COVID vaccine centre. Starmer posted a video in which he commended the church on its work in the community, but had to hastily take it down and issue a grovelling apology, because he hadn't realised the church held to a biblical view on sexual morality. It seems it had never occurred to him that there would be churches that would still believe the Bible – surely we've all moved on.

In many people's eyes, your attitude to same-sex relationships is the deciding factor determining whether you are a good person or not. Tolerance isn't good enough. Love for the individuals is irrelevant. Nothing less than approval of the behaviour will do. That means the Bible is immoral and so too is anyone who believes it.

There are two things we will think about as we consider this subject.

GOD'S DESIGN IS SAFE

Every parent has had to instruct children on the importance of using things for their intended purpose. "No, don't use the remote control as a drumstick – that's not what it was made for." "Don't use the cricket bat as a hammer – you are wrecking the bat – it wasn't made for that."

Human beings aren't the accidental by-products of blind forces acting on mindless matter. There is a creator/designer. That means we have a purpose and, in order to preserve ourselves from damage, we need to know what that purpose is, and align ourselves with it.

There are some items whose purpose is obvious – you just have to look at them and you can see what they are for. With other items, their purpose isn't so obvious. You would need to read the manufacturer's instructions to know what the thing is for. When it comes to human beings, there is an obvious purpose and we also have the manufacturer's instructions.

It is obvious that men and women are made for each other. There is a physical compatibility that just so happens to be the means of producing new life. It seems obvious that men were not designed to go with men, nor women with women. When we look at the manufacturer's instructions (the Bible), it confirms what nature loudly proclaims. When we use something in a way it wasn't made to be used, we wreck it.

Despite intense political pressure, the studies still show that same-sex relationships are harmful. The physical harm is obvious, but the emotional harm is clearly documented too. Often this emotional harm is attributed to social stigma and homophobia, but the medical literature says otherwise. An extensive study of those involved in same-sex relationships in the Netherlands found that they had higher rates of nearly all psychiatric pathologies mentioned in the study.[11] The Netherlands is one of the most "gay-affirming" places in the world, and so this study undermines the view that social disapproval lies at the root of the mental health problems of those involved in same-sex relationships.

God's laws are for the flourishing of humanity. The monogamous, exclusive, life-long, loving union of a man and woman in marriage is for the emotional, physical and psychological wellbeing of both involved, and any children that result from that union, and for the good of society. Any deviation from God's plan carries huge risks. God has placed boundaries around sex because of His compassion. There is safety in following God's design.

---

[11] Theo Sandfort, Ron de Graaf, et al., "Same-sex Sexual Behavior and Psychiatric Disorders," *Archives of General Psychiatry*.

GOD'S DESIGN IS SYMBOLIC

Marriage communicates a message. The union of a man and a woman in marriage symbolises the union of Christ and His church (Ephesians 5:25-27), so any tampering with that distorts something very precious to God.

The parallel between marriage and the relationship of Christ and His church is powerful. When a woman gets married, she takes a new name, she has a new identity. One of the reasons people find the Bible's condemnation of homosexual behaviour so offensive is to do with this matter of identity. The Bible condemns all sorts of behaviour that all of us are guilty of, but, when people point out that the Bible condemns lying, greed, fornication and adultery, there are no howls of protest or cries for anyone to lose their job. The reason is no one identifies himself as a liar, a greedy person, fornicator or adulterer. These things aren't key to our identity. But when it's pointed out that the Bible condemns homosexual behaviour there is an outcry because many engaged in that behaviour see it as a key part of who they are. The "love the sinner, hate the sin" distinction doesn't work with them, because they identify themselves by the thing the Bible calls sin, and so they say you can't hate the sin without hating them, and you can't love them without loving the sin.

The gospel offers a new, bigger, better identity. It calls on us to take up the cross, which means (among other things) that we accept God's verdict of condemnation.

He condemns not just our sexual sins, but our arrogant assumption that we have the authority to make our own rules and create our own identity apart from Him. When we repent of our rebellion and accept Christ as our only hope of salvation, He gives us a source of meaning and a sense of value that we all long for but look for in the wrong places. Salvation brings us into a union with Christ in which we find love, security, community and fellowship; and this provides the resources to enable us to let go of the idols that we thought we could never live without, the identity that once defined us.

The Bible's teaching on sex is not oppressive. It's not cruel. It's liberating and kind.

MISOGYNY

Back in 2012, the Church of England voted down legislation to approve women bishops. The Prime Minister, David Cameron, expressed his frustration, saying that the Church needed to "get with the programme". They did, of course, "get with the programme" a couple of years later, and so have many other churches. A few churches here and there still haven't got on board. Why is that? Well, they recognise that the job of a local church is not to get with the programme set by politicians or society. There is another programme that Christians are called to follow, and it is laid out in Scripture. Because of this, they, and the Bible, have been charged with misogyny, i.e., "dislike of, contempt for, or ingrained prejudice against, women". This is a serious charge. Is the Bible guilty? Hardly. Let's look at the facts.

The Bible asserts that men and women are *equal in value* but *different in role*.

EQUAL IN VALUE

Genesis 1:26-27 emphasises that men and women are both created in the image of God.

> *Then God said, "Let Us make man in Our image, according to Our likeness; let them have dominion over the fish of the sea, over the birds of the air, and over the cattle, over all the earth and over every creeping thing that creeps on the earth." So God created man in His own image; in the image of God He created him; male and female He created them.*

The very first chapter of the Bible establishes that women are equal in worth to men.

Genesis 2 teaches that God made one woman for one man – the relationship was to be committed and exclusive. Polygamy was not God's will, and the Bible's recording of it is only intended to show how harmful it is. Everywhere it is found it is shown to be bad.

> *From Lamech's wives to those of Abraham, Esau, Jacob, David, and Solomon, wherever we see God's ideal of monogamy ignored, we witness strife, competition, and disharmony. The Old Testament presents polygamy as not only undesirable but also a violation of God's standards. Old Testament narratives subtly critique this marital arrangement.*[12]

When we look at the New Testament, we see that the Lord Jesus was countercultural in His interactions with

---

[12]   Paul Copan, *Is God a Moral Monster?*, p. 117.

36

women. For example, He had women amongst His band of followers (Matthew 12:49-50; Luke 8:1-3) and He let Mary of Bethany sit at His feet with the men and be instructed by Him, rather than send her to help Martha with the cooking (Luke 10:38-42). Eliezer, a first century rabbi, said that if anyone teaches his daughter the Law (of Moses) it is as if he taught her promiscuity, and it would be better to burn the Law than teach it to a woman. Christ did not share that view. We find Christian women had valuable roles in the life of the early church (e.g., Acts 18:26; Romans 16; Philippians 4:2-3). The gospel teaches that there is no distinction between the standing of men and women before God in Christ. In fact, Paul says all Christians (male and female) are sons of God. Some take that to be sexist, but the very opposite is the case. In that culture, the sons, not the daughters, shared in the family business and got the inheritance. Paul is saying that every Christian has that position before God.

"For you are all sons of God through faith in Christ Jesus . . . There is neither Jew nor Greek, there is neither slave nor free, there is neither male nor female; for you are all one in Christ Jesus" (Galatians 3:26,28).

BUT WHAT ABOUT . . . ?

That all sounds good, but there are some passages that certainly appear to demean women. Let's have a look.

Leviticus 12:1-8

This passage teaches that a woman is ceremonially unclean for 40 days after giving birth to a boy, but 80 days after giving birth to a girl. So, are girls twice as unclean as boys? Given what we have already looked at, this is a very weak basis to argue for the Bible being misogynistic. There are various explanations for this law. The period of ceremonial uncleanness meant the mother couldn't come to the temple, and the fact that this was twice as long for the mother of a girl rather than a boy is taken by some to communicate a message of special protection for girls rather than boys – the mum was given twice as long off before she was expected to get back into normal life. Others suggest this law communicated that, in contrast to the nations around with their fertility cults and temple prostitutes, the temple wasn't the sphere of women's operation in Israel.

> Another plausible explanation focuses on a natural source of uncleanness – namely, the flow of blood. Verse 5 refers to the reason: it's because of 'the blood of her purification.' The mother experiences vaginal bleeding at birth. Yet such vaginal bleeding is common in newborn girls as well, due to the withdrawal of the mother's estrogen when the infant girl exits the mother's womb. So we have two sources of ritual uncleanness with a girl's birth but only one with a boy's.[13]

[13]   Copan, *Is God a Moral Monster?*, p. 106 (emphases his).

And once the time of purification is over, an identical purification offering is to be made whether it is for a son or a daughter, showing that females aren't viewed as being more defiled than males.

Leviticus 27:1-8

In this section we learn how people could show their willingness to serve Him, even though they couldn't actively serve in and for the tabernacle (because they weren't Levites). In lieu of their service they could give an equivalent value. But males are valued at more than females – does this not mean women are less valuable than men? This is to do with work connected to the tabernacle, and, generally speaking, men have higher economic marketability than women for manual labour. Clearly it isn't a statement on one's value as a person because a female aged between twenty and sixty has a higher price than a male in an older age bracket, and that obviously does not mean that the ancient Israelites thought older men had less worth than younger women. This was a society that extolled the value of the elderly, but it recognised that when it came to manual labour, there was more output from younger women than older men. Similarly (and this shouldn't be controversial), there is more manual output from men than from women of similar ages (generally). Some footballers are worth more than others, but this isn't a statement of their worth as *people* but as *footballers*. Similarly, this isn't a statement on the worth of men and women as people but as workers in the tabernacle.

Exodus 20:17

The tenth commandment forbids coveting what belongs to someone else. It says you aren't to covet your neighbour's house, wife, servant, ox, donkey or anything that belongs to him. The implication is that a wife is lumped in the same category as house, servant, ox and donkey, as being the property of the man. But a woman does belong to her husband *in the very same way* a husband is said to belong to his wife (e.g., Genesis 3:6; Song of Solomon 6:3). Wives, unlike houses, oxen and donkeys, could not be sold. The fifth commandment states that mothers are to be honoured as well as fathers, but in other cultures in the ancient Near East mothers were under the control of the son. Mothers are certainly not viewed as chattels. The teaching throughout the Bible (see especially the book of Proverbs) is that mothers are to be revered and listened to.

Marrying your rapist?

> "If a man finds a young woman who is a virgin, who is not betrothed, and he seizes her and lies with her, and they are found out, then the man who lay with her shall give to the young woman's father fifty shekels of silver, and she shall be his wife because he has humbled

her; he shall not be permitted to divorce her all his days" (Deuteronomy 22:28-29).

This passage seems unthinkably harsh, but there's more to it than meets the eye. First, marriage in that time was about survival (building a family to defend and care for you) and carrying on the family name. There weren't the romantic notions we connect with it now. Indeed, our view of marriage is in large part due to the gospel's influence – it presents itself as a love story, and encourages husbands to love their wives as Christ loves the church.

Also, Exodus 22:16-17 needs to be read in conjunction with this, because the Deuteronomy passage is seen by scholars as being an expansion of what was said in Exodus 22.

> *If a man entices a virgin who is not betrothed, and lies with her, he shall surely pay the bride-price for her to be his wife. If her father utterly refuses to give her to him, he shall pay money according to the bride-price of virgins.*

The point here is that the father of the young woman (no doubt in consultation with her) can refuse to let the marriage take place. If he did so then the man was to pay a sizeable bridal price to ensure some measure of financial security for a woman who would find it harder now to find a husband. If this stipulation was in place for a woman who had been enticed, then that stipulation would certainly be in place for a woman who had been seized, so there is no forced marriage here.

> This case is similar to the one mentioned in Exodus 22:16-17. The omission to mention the possibility of the father refusing to give him his daughter for a wife, makes no essential difference. It is assumed as self-evident here, that such a right was possessed by the father.[14]

It should also be noted that the word that indicates rape is not used in Deuteronomy 22:28-29. It is used in verse 25: "But if a man finds a betrothed young woman in the countryside, and the man forces her and lies with her, then only the man who lay with her shall die." The word in verse 28 is a weaker word that is more in keeping with the thought of seduction. The fact that it says, "and *they* are found out" indicates culpability on the part of the woman as well, but only the man is held responsible.

A woman who was not a virgin would have had her chances for marriage severely reduced, and that is why when Amnon raped Tamar she begged him to marry her (2 Samuel 13:7-18). We don't have the right to enforce our ideals of marriage retrospectively on people who would

---

[14] C. F. Keil, *Commentary on the Book of Deuteronomy* in C. F. Keil and F. Delitzsch, *Commentary on the Old Testament*, Volume 1, Hendrickson, 2006, p. 947.

have probably looked on them as a bit silly. The man was responsible to take and provide for the woman he had violated and never divorce her – she would be secure for the rest of her life.

We don't see a lack of concern for the woman in this passage. As Paul Copan says, "Her well-being is actually the underlying theme of this legislation."[15]

No female priests

There was a *practical* reason for this – the surrounding cultures had female priests and their function was to engage in sexual immorality. The nation of Israel was different. They exemplified their separation from the perversity of the surrounding cultures in lots of ways, and one was no female priests.

There was also a *prophetical* reason for this – the priesthood was one of the three anointed offices of Israel (the offices of king and prophet were the others). Every priest was a picture of *The Anointed One* – the Christ who would come - and so, the priesthood was reserved for the males.

Then finally, there was a *patriarchal* reason for this – the priests were the leaders and teachers in Israel, and, like it or not, God's will is that the man functions as the leader. This brings us to our next major subject. Although men and women are equal in value, they are different in role.

---

[15] Copan, *Is God a Moral Monster?*, p. 119.

DIFFERENT IN ROLE

The Bible teaches that men and women have different God-given roles and spheres of responsibility. The man is placed by God in a position of leadership (see 1 Timothy 2:12-13). This was reflected in Old Testament Israel (the priestly office was held by men), and in the Gospels (the Lord selected twelve men as His apostles). It is also to be reflected in the New Testament church. The Bible teaches that the head of the woman is the man (1 Corinthians 11:3). This does not imply inferiority because the same verse states that the head of Christ is God, yet the Bible teaches Christ is equal with God (Philippians 2:6). The headship of man is to be demonstrated in leadership and teaching in the church (1 Timothy 2:11-12), and the woman observing the symbol of head covering while the man's head is uncovered (1 Corinthians 11:4-16).

This is offensive to many, but there are many things the Bible teaches that people find offensive – the fault isn't with the Bible, it is with our arrogant assumption that our culture is right. Throughout history every culture has had problems with the Bible, including the culture in which the Bible was written. This is because, although the Bible was written within a culture, it was not sourced in that culture. The things that our culture struggles with are not the things other cultures have had difficulties with. For example, the average person in Britain today would approve of the Bible's teaching on loving and forgiving your enemies, but would have big issues with the Bible's teaching on hell, but in the Britain of 1,000 years ago the opposite was the case. The idea of loving and forgiving one's enemy didn't fit well within an honour and shame culture, but the idea of hell fitted quite comfortably. It is what C. S. Lewis called "chronological snobbery" to give "uncritical acceptance of the intellectual climate common to our own age and the assumption that whatever has gone out of date is on that account discredited."[16]

Up until the very recent past, everyone recognised that women are better fitted for some roles and men for others. This is not oppression but reality. And it shows up when we aren't thinking about it. For example, when the husband hears a clatter downstairs during the night, he doesn't say to his wife, "It's your turn to go down and check; I did it the last time." That's an "equality" that no one insists on or wants. It is the role of the man to put himself in danger for his wife and family. Likewise, God has given the man the responsibility of leadership.

The real misogyny is not from those who recognise the unique glory women have, but from those who say that women have to suppress their God-given instincts, despise their uniqueness, and try to behave like men.

A lot of churches have heeded David Cameron's call to "get with the programme." However, God has another

---

[16]   C. S. Lewis, *Surprised by Joy.*

programme. The roles of men and women reflect the love story of Christ and His church. So, rather than being stuck in the past, biblical gender roles portray the eternal future.

BIGOTRY

It's possible to give a right answer but leave a wrong impression. That was driven home to me one day as I overheard a conversation between a Christian and a woman who would have described herself as spiritual but not religious. She said to the Christian, "So, what about all the Muslims and Hindus and Buddhists in the world? Are you saying they're all going to hell if they don't believe in Jesus?" The Christian replied, "Well, Christ said, 'I am the way, the truth, and the life. No one comes to the Father except through Me,' so that settles it."

Did he answer *accurately*? Are people who don't believe in Christ going to hell? Well, according to the Bible, yes. But he didn't answer *adequately*. He reinforced this woman's view that the God of the Bible is horrendously narrow-minded and bigoted – He doesn't care how well you live or how much you love, all He cares about is that you believe the right thing. No matter how good you are, if you fail your theology exam and pick the wrong religion, He throws you into hell, and no matter how bad you are, if you believe the right thing you go to heaven.

That sounds cruel and petty. It sounds like God is the captain of a cruise ship who threatens to throw the passengers overboard unless they accept a lifebelt from him. But that isn't the biblical picture. An illustration that is more in keeping with the teaching of the Bible is that we are the crew of an enemy ship that has been attacking this captain's ship; our ship has gone down and we are drowning. The captain throws the lifebelt out to us. Rejecting the lifebelt doesn't *put* us in danger, it *keeps* us in danger. The lifebelt isn't the problem, it's the answer.

So it is with Christ. Accepting Him isn't some arbitrary hoop that God makes us jump through. He is the only answer to the problem we have. Let's look at the problem and then we'll see how Jesus is the only possible answer.

THE PROBLEM

The problem we face is that we have sinned against God. Because God is righteous, sin must be dealt with. God can't turn a blind eye to our guilt. God's law flows from His nature, and thus cannot be set aside. The penalty for sin must be paid and God's wrath against it must be expressed.

We have broken God's law, and we can't unbreak it. Even if we could live a perfect life from now till the day we die, we are only doing what is demanded for the whole of our lives. Keeping the law in the future doesn't deal with our breaking of it in the past.

Back in the early 16th century, Martin Luther realised the problem. He was a man who had devoted his life to the service of God in an effort to placate Him by his religious devotions. But he said there was a phrase from the Bible "that had stood in my way". He said, "I hated that word, 'the righteousness of God." He realised that God's righteousness left the guilty with no hope of earning God's acceptance. All we could ever deserve was His wrath and judgement.

THE ANSWER

Our situation is completely hopeless . . . unless there is someone who is able and willing to stand in our place, to act as our representative, and bear the judgement for us. If there is someone like that, then there would be a way of salvation. And that is why Jesus is the only way. He was eternally one with God, and He became one with us – coming into the human family so that He could act on our behalf and bear the sin of the world. That's what He did on the cross. He paid the penalty in full, and proved it by His resurrection, and now there is a way that a righteous God can accept sinners without compromising His righteousness. God can't accept me on the basis of the life I have lived, but He can accept me on the basis of the death Christ died. Through repentance and faith in Christ, I am united to Him, and God accepts what Christ did as being in my place, and I go free.

Greg Koukl put it like this:

Mankind faces a singular problem. People are broken and the world is broken because our friendship with

God has been broken, ruined by human rebellion. Humans, you and I – are guilty, enslaved, lost, dead. All of us. Everyone. Everywhere. The guilt must be punished, the debt must be paid, the slave must be purchased. Promising better conduct in the future will not mend the crimes of the past. No, a rescuer must ransom the slaves, a kindred brother must pay the family debt, a substitute must shoulder the guilt. There is no other way of escape. This is why Jesus of Nazareth is the only way to God, the only possible source of rescue. He is the only one who solved the problem. No other man did this. No other person could. Not Mohammed. Not the Buddha. Not Krishna. Not anyone else. Only Jesus of Nazareth could save the world. Without him we are crushed under our overwhelming debt. Without him, every single one of us would have to pay for our own crimes, and that would take eternity.[17]

People aren't going to hell because God is annoyed they picked the wrong religion. People are going to hell because they are guilty of breaking His law. Religion offers no answer for our guilt. Christ is the answer – He is the Saviour. If that Saviour is refused, then there is no other option but that we remain in our danger.

[17]   Gregory Koukl, *The Story of Reality, How the World Began, How it Ends, and Everything Important that Happens in Between*, Zondervan, 2017, p. 132.

God has thrown a lifebelt out to a perishing world. As long as people think they can swim to safety themselves, they will reject Christ. Once they realise they are helpless, they will see He is the only hope.

CRUELTY

Context is important. If I told you I saw a man running up to an unsuspecting little boy and rugby tackling him, breaking the boy's arm in the process, you might want to know whether the man was reported to the police.

However, a bit of context changes the picture – the boy had wandered into the road and the man saved his life. What seemed cruel is now shown to be noble and good. We need to make sure we have all the facts before we rush to condemnation.

This is especially true when it comes to condemning the Bible. A lot of people are in a hurry to condemn the God revealed in Scripture as cruel, based on a shallow understanding of out-of-context passages.

The God of the Bible is a God whose nature is love (1 John 4:8), and this isn't just the "sanitised" New Testament version. In every part of the Old Testament (the Law, the Psalms and the Prophets) we see the consistent revelation of a God who is slow to anger, abounding in love and ready to forgive (e.g., Exodus 34:6-7; Psalm 86:5; Jonah 4:2), who cares for the stranger, the widow and the fatherless (e.g., Deuteronomy 14:28-29; 27:19; Psalm 68:5; 146:9; Jeremiah 7:6-7).

So, what do we make then of the passages that make us wince? Before diving into the particulars let's remember three things. First of all, God is the only possible foundation for morality. It makes no sense to talk about God being unjust, because that implies there is a standard of justice outside of God that He has to conform to. God *is* the standard of goodness. Anything He does is, by definition, right. Secondly, the Bible has proven itself to be God's Word.[18] If, therefore, we find something in it that seems wrong, then either *we* are wrong or *our interpretation* is wrong; what can't be the case is that God's Word is wrong. Thirdly, God has revealed Himself fully in Christ (John 1:18; Hebrews 1:1-3). If you want to know exactly what God is like, look at Jesus – He tells the full story and gives the complete picture.

Let's now look at a couple of issues that people think are examples of cruelty on God's part:

1. Capital punishments
2. Eternal punishment

CAPITAL PUNISHMENTS

One particularly troubling example of capital punishment being carried out is the execution of Achan and his family

---

[18] For more on this see Paul McCauley, *Prove It, How you can know and show that the Bible is God's word*, Decapolis Press, 2017, or https://understandingthegospel.org/explore-the-gospel/the-bible/.

in Joshua 7. Against God's command, Achan took spoil from the city of Jericho. When this came to light, Achan and his family were stoned to death. There are three issues to deal with:

1. Why would God want anyone to be stoned to death?
2. Why would God want Achan to be stoned to death?
3. Why would God want Achan's family to be stoned to death?

1. WHY WOULD GOD WANT ANYONE TO BE STONED TO DEATH?

It seems such a brutal means of execution, why would God not institute something more humane as a death penalty? There are a few things to keep in mind – first, it was a brutal world, life was hard, and people were a lot less squeamish about such things back then. It is the transforming power of the gospel in culture that has resulted in us looking at such things with such horror. In lands where the gospel's impact has not been widely known or deeply felt, there still is such brutality. As we said in a previous chapter, there were provisions in the Mosaic law that were included, not because they reflected God's perfect ideal, but "because of the hardness of your hearts" (Matthew 19:8). Secondly, the penalty was supposed to act as a deterrent, and it clearly did. In the records of Israel's early history we have a few instances of the penalty being legitimately carried out (Leviticus 24:10-23; Numbers 15:30-36; Joshua 7), and that is it – the marker had been laid down; God is serious about this, and the people got the message: "all Israel shall hear and fear" (Deuteronomy 21:21). Thirdly, it was a collective form of execution – it was the whole congregation of Israel that was responsible for putting the offender to death. They didn't have an executioner. This heightened the solemnity of the issue and helped drive the message home.

God knows better than we do what is required in different circumstances. This was the sentence for certain crimes for the nation of Israel living under the Mosaic Covenant. It is not a command for all nations for all time. And let us remember, our society is really in no position to give God advice on just punishments and effective deterrents.

2. WHY WOULD GOD WANT ACHAN TO BE STONED TO DEATH?

What had Achan done that was so serious? Well, this was Israel's first battle after crossing Jordan into the Promised Land; God had given a specific command that nothing was to be taken from Jericho for themselves – it was all devoted to destruction (Joshua 6:17-19). Achan's sin was an act of direct rebellion. The nation of Israel was being used by God to purge the land of Canaan of its idolatry and immorality; it would therefore be hypocritical of

God to permit an idolatrous and immoral man to inflict judgement on the Canaanites.

3. WHY WOULD GOD WANT ACHAN'S FAMILY TO BE STONED TO DEATH?

God's law forbids children from being executed for the crimes of their fathers:

> "Fathers shall not be put to death for their children,
> nor shall children be put to death for their fathers;
> a person shall be put to death for his own sin"
> (Deuteronomy 24:16).

This establishes that Achan's family were complicit in his crime. After all, if someone buries a robe, 200 pieces of silver and a bar of gold in his tent, it is pretty obvious that the other people who live in the tent will know about it. It is not the case then that his family were innocent parties. They shared in the punishment because they shared in the guilt.

ETERNAL PUNISHMENT

"Seventy years of sin, eternal punishment?! Talk about an overreaction! The punishment doesn't fit the crime. Seventy years of sin should result in seventy years of punishment – an eye for an eye." This was the content of a (very understandable) rant from a man I was speaking to. There are two things I think we should bear in mind as we look at this subject.

a) The infinite holiness of God

I suggested to the man I was speaking to that his reasoning wasn't altogether sound. We don't base punishment for crimes on how long it took to commit them. I asked him how long it took to commit a murder. Say it takes someone a week to plan and carry it out, are we suggesting that an appropriate punishment for the murderer is a week in prison? See the problem? The punishment is not based on the time it took to commit the crime but on the gravity of the crime.

When we look at it like that it is no surprise that the Bible teaches eternal punishment. God is infinitely holy and sin-hating. Every sin defies His authority and also defaces His image. He has created us in His image, as His representatives, and when we sin we demean Him. "Hell is God's declaration to the universe that what every sin demeans is of infinite worth."[19] To sin against Him is to commit a crime of infinite seriousness which carries with it an infinite penalty. That is why the punishment lasts forever – as finite creatures we can never pay an infinite penalty.

---

[19] John Piper, *Jesus: The Only Way to God – Must You Hear the Gospel to be Saved?*, Baker Books, 2010, p. 32.

b) The intrinsic value of man

J. P. Moreland said:

> Believe it or not, everlasting separation from God is morally superior to annihilation...Why would God be morally justified in annihilating somebody? The only way that's a good thing would be the end result, which would be to keep people from experiencing the conscious separation from God forever. Well, then you're treating people as a means to an end...What hell does is recognise that people have intrinsic value. If God loves intrinsic value, then He has got to be a sustainer of persons, because that means He is a sustainer of intrinsic value. He refuses to snuff out a creature that was made in His own image. So in the final analysis, hell is the only morally legitimate option.[20]

If people don't want God, then they will be exiled from Him, but not extinguished by Him. In the end, they get what they want – separation from God. And even if they could pay the penalty for past crimes (which they can't), their ongoing rebellion necessitates ongoing punishment.[21]

---

[20] Lee Strobel, *The Case for Faith*, Zondervan, 2000, p. 255.
[21] For more on this, see Paul McCauley, *He that believeth not*, John Ritchie Ltd, 2013.

CONCLUSION

Lamentations 3:33 tells us, "For He does not afflict willingly [literally, *from His heart*], nor grieve the children of men." God takes no pleasure in human suffering. He only allows it when it is necessary, and, in order to save us from the eternal punishment we deserve, He willingly bore the penalty for us on the cross. Such a God is worthy of our trust – He is good.

WEIRDNESS

Don't eat pork or shellfish, don't wear clothes of mixed fabrics, don't sow your vineyard with different kinds of seed, don't shave the edges of your beard . . . That is a sample of the commands God gave in His law that strike many today as . . . well, weird.

Why would anyone, never mind God, care about these things? And, if Christians are meant to take the Bible as being God's Word, why don't any of them obey these laws? Does this not show that Christians pick and choose which parts of the Bible to obey?

There are a couple of things to bear in mind:

1. These commands weren't for everyone – *they were for a certain people*
2. These commands weren't for ever – *they were for a certain period*

As we look at these two subjects, we will see that these commands *were for a certain purpose*, and that purpose has been fulfilled.

These commands weren't for everyone – *they were for a certain people*

God selected Israel as the nation through which the Messiah would come. It was vital then that they be kept separate from the nations around to maintain the purity of their God-given religion and the integrity of their genealogies. Mixing with the surrounding idolatrous nations was an existential threat to the mission of Israel, and so God emphasised the lesson of separation in every sphere of their lives. In the foods they ate, in the clothes they wore, in the seeds they planted, even in the way they groomed their faces – God was saying, "Don't mix, stay separate."

Animals were classified as clean or unclean, and there have been interesting reasons suggested as to why certain animals would be classed as unclean and not allowed for food. Scholars have shown that the forbidden animals were predatory animals, animals that fed on unclean things, or animals that exhibited a lack (i.e., they were defective in some symbolically significant way). In the Bible, eating is symbolic for what we feed our minds on, and what shapes our character. With this in mind, we see that the Lord is communicating that He doesn't want His people being predatory, unclean or defective in their character.[22]

The prohibition on mixing fabrics and sowing with different kinds of seeds (Deuteronomy 22:9-12) enforced the lesson that in everyday life and in business life the Israelites were to be separate from the surrounding nations.

---

[22] For more on this, see Copan, *Is God a Moral Monster?*, pp. 80-84.

The instruction not to mark their beards (Leviticus 19:27) had to do with not following heathen occultic practices (as Leviticus 19:28 indicates). According to the historian Herodotus, the Arab tribes marked their beards in certain ways in honour of their gods.

There are other "strange" laws, but what we have looked at should satisfy us that they were given because of their symbolic significance. While in some cases their significance might escape us, the Israelites would likely have understood the point – God wanted them to be distinct.

These commands weren't for ever –
they were for a certain period

We have established that one purpose of the ceremonial law was to separate Israel from the nations. Another purpose of the ceremonial law was to point forward to Christ. For example, the animal sacrifices had no saving value, but they pointed forward to the sacrifice of the Lord Jesus, and all the details connected to these offerings have wonderful significance and fulfilment in Him.

When we see this twofold purpose of the ceremonial law (to make Israel distinct and to point forward to Christ), we can see that they have served their purpose. The Messiah has come – the ceremonies have been fulfilled. The dividing wall between Israel and the nations has been broken down and God has started something new – the Church – composed of all believers, no matter their nationality:

"For He Himself is our peace, who has made both one, and has broken down the middle wall of separation, having abolished in His flesh the enmity, that is, the law of commandments contained in ordinances, so as to create in Himself one new man from the two, thus making peace, and that He might reconcile them both to God in one body through the cross, thereby putting to death the enmity" (Ephesians 2:14-16).

The law of Moses was for the nation of Israel (a certain people) under the Old Covenant (a certain period). So, does that mean we dispense with all the commandments of the Mosaic law? Do we say that *none* of the commands is binding? No. Not at all. Many of the commands are binding, but *not because they are in the law of Moses*. If you looked at the laws of another country, some of those laws would be applicable to you, but only because they are also the laws of the country *you* live in. The law of Moses is the law of another country, but many of the commandments are relevant to all humanity – God has written them on the hearts of all men (Romans 2:15). We can see that the moral aspects of the law were not just for a certain people, because God said He was judging the nations for their abominations:

"Do not defile yourselves with any of these things; for by all these the nations are defiled, which I am casting out before you. For the land is defiled; therefore I visit

the punishment of its iniquity upon it, and the land vomits out its inhabitants" (Leviticus 18:24-25).

These nations weren't guilty of transgressing the Mosaic law (it hadn't been given), but they were guilty of transgressing the law God had written on their hearts.

We see too when we come into the New Testament that the moral aspects of the law weren't for a certain period. Eating pork was wrong under the law of Moses, but when that covenant ended the eating of pork was no longer wrong. However, murder, lying, adultery, etc. are still wrong, and condemned in the New Testament.

These strange ceremonial aspects of the law, while not binding on anyone today, are certainly not irrelevant. When we look at them through the lens of the culture Israel was in there are big lessons for us to learn about the holiness God desires from His people, and when we look at them through the lens of the gospel there are wonderful truths for us to discover about the Saviour who is pictured in so many of these passages.

THE FINAL WORD

Imagine you are travelling home one night in your car. You are going through a dangerous part of a big city and you run out of petrol. You have to get out and walk to the nearest petrol station. As you are walking through the dark streets you see a group of young men coming down the street towards you. Would you be more scared or less if you found out that they were Christians who had just been having a Bible study?

My guess is you would be breathing a sigh of relief. You would be saying, "If they take the Bible seriously then I have nothing to fear from them." You see, despite all the people claiming the Bible is evil, when we look at the real world, the facts tell a very different story.

Investigate the cause of the great social reforms throughout history, the origin of charities, the roots of health care and hospitals, the birth of modern science, the founding of schools and universities, etc. You will find that the motivation for it all has been the teaching of the Bible.[23]

---

[23] For more on this see Alvin J. Schmidt, *How Christianity Changed the World*, Zondervan, kindle edition 2009 or Sharon James, *How Christianity Transformed the World*, Christian Focus, 2021.

For those who dream of a society free from the Bible's influence, all they have to do is waken up and study history, and then they would realise it would be a nightmare. Look at any country that has been changed by the biblical gospel – is the change for the better or the worse? Does anyone want to go back to the superstition, the cruelty, the human sacrifices and widow-burnings of these pre-Christian cultures? How have societies fared that have sought to eliminate the influence of the Bible? Was the Soviet Union the utopia its founders envisaged it would be?

In 2016, the conclusion of a two-volume symposium published by Cambridge University Press was that:

> . . . free institutions hardly ever developed in places that were not influenced by Jewish and Christian ideas [i.e., biblical ideas]. Outside the Judeo-Christian tradition, it has been rare for thinkers to suppose that God endowed us with a nature of our own, that freedom is part of that nature . . .[24]

Alvin Schmidt points out:

> The very freedom of speech and expression that ironically permits them to castigate Christian values is largely a by-product of Christianity's influences that

---

[24] *Christianity and Freedom*, Cambridge University Press, cited in James, *How Christianity Transformed the World*.

have been incorporated into the social fabric of the Western world.[25]

Where the biblical gospel prospers, society prospers.

The Bible's positive effect on societies is because of its positive effect on individuals. Yes, there are many people who claim to believe the Bible yet live self-centred lives, but we have a word for them – hypocrites. We don't say that such people are good examples of biblical teaching, but contradictions of it. Even if you have had negative experiences with Christians, my guess is that you do know some people who are the real deal – people whose lives have been powerfully and positively transformed, not by determination or religion, but by the message of the Bible. A book that carries this power and makes such a difference is a book that is worth investigating. As the old saying goes, the proof of the pudding is in the eating, and this is a metaphor the Bible uses – swallow its teachings and see what happens:

> "The law of the Lord is perfect, converting the soul; the testimony of the Lord is sure, making wise the simple; the statutes of the Lord are right, rejoicing the heart; the commandment of the Lord is pure, enlightening the eyes; the fear of the Lord is clean, enduring forever; the judgments of the Lord are true and righteous altogether. More to be desired are they than gold, yea,

[25] Schmidt, *How Christianity Changed the World*, loc 228.

than much fine gold; sweeter also than honey and the honeycomb. Moreover by them Your servant is warned, and in keeping them there is great reward" (Psalm 19:7-11).

People will accuse Christians of picking and choosing when it comes to the Bible. They will say, "You are focussing on the good bits and ignoring the bad." No, it is the critic, not the Christian, who is picking and choosing. The critic is the one combing through the Bible looking for shock quotes. As we have seen in these chapters, when these tough passages are examined in their scriptural and historical context, and we look carefully at the content and intent of the text, another picture and a different story emerge.

The picture the Bible gives of God is that He is eternally loving, the source and standard of truth, goodness and beauty. The story of the Bible is that this God created us for fellowship with Himself; our rebellion has separated us from Him, and He has made the way back through His Son, and seeks to bring us back through His Spirit, so that we can be free from the penalty and power of sin, and enjoy the love and relationship we were created to enjoy, forever. *That* is a good book.

If you are a critic of the Bible, make sure you are an honest critic – the Bible is a book with a vast amount of evidence supporting it, and with millions of people willing to testify to its life-changing power. Read the Bible again, this time not to find out what's wrong with it, but to find out what's wrong with you. Open yourself up to it. See the big picture; get the main message, and everything else falls into place.

The attacks on the Bible will keep coming, and one reason for that is that the Bible isn't going anywhere. It is "the word of God which lives and abides forever" (1 Peter 1:23). So, as long as there are rebels on earth there will be attacks against Scripture, but when the rebellion is defeated and the rebels exiled, the Word of God will stand.

ND - #0173 - 250324 - C0 - 198/129/5 - PB - 9781787988989 - Gloss Lamination